BEFORE YOU ST

MACBETH

In this section you will find some background information to help you understand a little more about Shakespeare's time and the language he used in his plays. It is designed to help you jump back over 350 years to when the play was written.

A. THE TRAGEDIE OF MACBETH.

B.

MACBETH
Majesty's Theatre

C.

D.

Is this a clanger I see before me?
Timothy West attacks O'Toole
and disowns Old Vic production

DAGGERS OUT FOR MACBETH

by Michael Owen
ACTOR Peter O'Toole stayed silent
today at the centre of an extra-

A. The first page of Macbeth
   as it was printed in 1623.
B. A theatre poster from the
   turn of the century.
C. Shooting a scene from
   Roman Polanski's 1971
   film Macbeth.
D. A newspaper headline the
   day after a new production of Macbeth opened in
   London - September 1980.

SHAKESPEARE'S LANGUAGE

The moment you begin to read a play by William Shakespeare you will notice the language. If you have not read it before it may seem old-fashioned, complicated, confusing and difficult. Most people find Shakespeare's language difficult so don't be discouraged if you find it hard going at first.

You do have to work hard on Shakespeare's plays, but you will find that the effort is more than worth it. Once you have made a start you will find that it gets easier. As it becomes easier to read, you will realize that Shakespeare's plays are packed full of excitement, humour, sadness, despair, sex, violence, tragedy, treachery, bravery, cowardice, trickery and grand passions.

Once you become familiar with two or three plays you will understand why many people say that Shakespeare was the most brilliant writer England has ever had or is likely to have.

It will help you to stick with it if you have a clearer understanding of why the language in Macbeth looks so confusing to begin with.

The first reason is the most obvious.

Shakespeare wrote his plays over 350 years ago. Language changes all the time. Even so-called modern slang becomes old-fashioned in a few years. In the 1960's everything was *fab* and *gear* and *far out*. Now here are a whole range of different words. Language is bound to change a great deal in 350 years.

Here is Ben Jonson writing in 1601 (a couple of years before Macbeth was written). He is attacking the trendy new habit of smoking:

By gods me: I marvel what pleasure or felicitie they have in taking this rogish Tabacco; it's good for nothing but to choke a man, and fill him full of smoake and embers; there were foure died out of one house last weeke with taking it, and two more the bell went for yester-night, one of them (they say) will ne'er escape it, he voyded a bushell of soote yesterday, upward and downward. I'ld have it present death, man or woman, that should but dele with a tabacco pipe; why it will stifle them all in the end as many as use it; it's little better than rat's bane.
From 'Every Man in His Humor', 1601.

That gives you an idea of what English sounded like in 1600. It is different, but you probably understood most of it, especially if you read it aloud.

The reason Shakespeare's language is even more difficult to understand than normal speech of the time, is that he wanted the characters in his plays to express themselves in *poetry*. You will know from the modern poetry you have read, that poems can be more difficult than prose.

Not only is Shakespeare writing in a language used 350 years ago, but he is also using it in a poetic way.

You may want to ask: Why did he go to all that trouble to write a poetic play if it means that I cannot understand a blind word he's saying?

The answer to that question may not seem very satisfactory to you: *he has written most of his play in a poetic way because he wants the language to sound better and say more.*

FOUR VERSIONS

Look at an example from the early part of the play. A messenger has come on stage to tell the King about a battle against some rebels. He wants to tell him how brave and valiant Macbeth has been in killing the rebel leader, MacDonald.

Here is a clear and simple version of what the messenger said:

1

Macbeth deserves to be called brave. He ignored all danger and went right across the battle field using his sword to kill anyone who got in his way. When he faced MacDonald he immediately killed him by cutting him in half with a single stroke, and cut off his head to put up on the castle wall.

Now, that tells the story. Most people who can read English would understand what happened. But there is a lot missing. You do not have to be an Elizabethan poet to improve the way that story has been told.

Here is how a West Indian living in Britain might tell a similar story:

2

Bredderin, lemme tell you
Macbeth him dread.
Him a real stiksman. Terrifyin dem Babylon rebels
He gotta a blade an' 'im use it.
Stabbin an slashin' all aroun im,
No one can deflec de man, him mek a way tru de rebel skank
He give dis MacDonald heavy liks
Lik 'im an lash im
an stab im
an kill im
Slash im belly from side to side
Carve off im head and stick in an him wall.
Dread warrior, righteous sticksman.

And here is the way a Cockney Londoner might tell the story:

3

Don't talk to me abaht MacBeth.
Wot a punter. Wot a performer.
He's yer akshul Ghengis Kahn on wheels.
I mean, this MacDonald, right sheister and no mistake.
Never stood a prayer, did he?
Macbeth's well tooled up. Lovely blade an' 'andy wiv it.
Seen the guts of more rebel oppos than you've 'ad hot dinners. Straight over there. No messin. Pins this MacDonald, no bovver.
Slits 'im from ear to ear an' back again.
Then, you can see he's got style, then he off's wiv his head and ups it on to the bleedin' parapet.
Well, I mean,
You gotta hand it to 'im.
A stylish punter wouln't you say guvnor?

What makes these versions different to the straight-forward description? You could call it the difference between poetry and plain writing.

If you aren't familiar with the Jamaican or Cockney dialect you might find it difficult to understand at first, but both versions have added a lot to the original. They make it *sound* better and *say* more.

Now look at how Shakespeare has dealt with the same scene:

4

> For brave Macbeth - well he deserves that name -
> Disdaining Fortune, with his brandish'd steel
> Which smok'd with bloody execution,
> Like valour's minion, carv'd out his passage
> Till he fac'd the slave;
> Which ne'er shook hands, nor bade farewell to him,
> Till he unseam'd him from the nave to th' chaps,
> And fix'd his head upon our battlements.

1.2.16

Remember that Shakespeare wrote that to be spoken out loud. Try reading it out loud. You should see what it means to *sound better*, especially if you then read version A. again. Which version leaves you with the most vivid picture in your mind?

It might help you to feel more familiar with Shakespeare's language if you did a similar exercise.

Here is a piece of Shakespeare's writing from later on in Macbeth. Lennox is describing the strange things that happened the night a murder was committed:

> *Lennox*
> The night has been unruly. Where we lay,
> Our chimneys were blown down; and, as they say,
> Lamentings heard i' th' air, strange screams of death
> And prophesying, with accents terrible,
> Of dire combustion and confus'd events
> New hatch'd to th' woeful time; the obscure bird
> Clamour'd the livelong night. Some say the earth
> Was feverous and did shake.

2.3.56

First: try to write a plain version of this speech. Just include the facts and nothing else.

Now try to write a version in a modern dialect you are familiar with.

SUPERSTITIONS AND FEARS

**WHO ARE THESE WOMEN?
WHAT IS HAPPENING TO THEM?**

They're being burned to death because it is believed they are witches. The devil has appeared in the form of a flying monster, and is speaking to one of them. As witches, they are suspected of having these evil powers:

They speak with the Devil, and with his help they can communicate with the dead. The most popular of them can see into the future.

They make people fall ill by using spells and potions, and can kill people at a distance.

(This drawing of the Devil was used in casting such spells.)

They can fly through the air, and can make themselves invisible at will.

(Here the witches are escaping up the chimney from someone who is trying to spy on them. They use ordinary brooms to ride on.)

They use animals such as cats as disguises for the evil spirits who serve them.

(Here the witches are meeting in secret, and can safely wear their magic hats. The evil spirit has taken its true shape.)

They can cause bad weather and storms, affecting ships at sea and spoiling the crops.

(These witches are making rain, using a spell that requires boiling up a chicken and a snake.)

THE FACTS: In Shakespeare's time most people believed that witches could do all these things. It's hard to believe, but hundreds of thousands of women were tortured and executed in Europe because they were accused of witchcraft. They were blamed for accidents, misfortunes and disasters of all kinds, and whole societies were sometimes whipped up into panic by the fear that evil forces were trying to destroy them.

When Shakespeare wrote *Macbeth*, the King of England was James I. He was personally terrified of witches, because he believed that a group of them (seen above being beaten to make them confess) had raised a storm to try to drown him, and then had made a wax image of him to make him sicken and die. They confessed, and were all executed. James I got Parliament to pass the following law.

That "if any person shall use any invocation or conjuration of any evil or wicked spirit; 2. or shal consult, covenant with, entertain, employ, feed or reward any evil or cursed spirit to or for any intent or purpose; 3. or take up any dead man, woman or child out of the grave, - or the skin, bone, or any part of the dead person, to be employed or used in any manner of witchcraft, sorcery, charm, or enchantment; 4. or shall use, practice, or exercise any sort of witchcraft, sorcery, charm or enchantment; 5. whereby any person shall be destroyed, killed, wasted, consumed, pined, or lamed in any part of the body; 6. that every such person being convicted shall suffer death."

The play *Macbeth* was probably performed for the first time at Hampton Court in 1605 or 1606. King James I would have been in the audience, and would have been delighted to see this play. Not only did it show that witches were real, and could be a danger to kings; it also told the story of the downfall of a man who killed a king. This would have been very reassuring to James I because he had recently survived, by a stroke of good luck, an attempt on his own life. This murder attempt is now called...

King James the First

THE GUNPOWDER PLOT

In 1605, a group of Catholic gentlemen tried to kill James I by blowing up the Houses of Parliament with barrels of gunpowder hidden in the cellar. The plot was discovered, and one of the leaders Guido (or Guy) Faukes (third from the right) was tortured and executed.

As you read the play, it is worth remembering that although the story may seem incredible to you, it dealt with matters that were all too real to the people who first watched it.

READING
MACBETH

This section is for use as you read the play in class, or follow the text
while listening to a record. It follows the play scene by scene, each with
the following notes:

THE HEADLINE
This will give you an idea of what the scene will be about. (Some do this
more successfully than others; you might want to think up your own).
This is followed by a brief description of what happens in the scene.

LINES TO LOOK OUT FOR
These are lines that often stick in the mind of someone reading the play, and
are worth stopping to discuss as you come to them. (Of course, they are not
the only lines worth discussing). If you can remember them as you read or
watch the play, they should help you to keep track of what is being said.

QUESTIONS
These deal with issues raised in the scene. They're not comprehension
questions; they're for thinking and talking about when you've read that
scene.

Each scene also has a picture taken from the television version of the
Royal Shakespeare Company's production of *Macbeth*. With each picture you will find some questions to help you think about how the play
might look and also consider what the director adds to a play in production. Remember these are television images of a stage production.

ACT 1

Scene 1

MEET THE WEIRD SISTERS

The three weird sisters plan to meet Macbeth after the battle.

LINES TO LOOK OUT FOR

a) When the battle's lost and won.

b) Fair is foul, and foul is fair.

QUESTIONS

Why do you think Shakespeare begins this play with the witches?

What does this scene tell you about the play that is to follow? What sort of play are you expecting?

The oldest sister is questioning the youngest. Can you suggest which line she is speaking at this moment? Can you explain why the younger sister appears to be in a trance? Is this how you imagined the weird sisters?

Scene 2

NEWS FROM THE BATTLEFIELD

a) A wounded captain has made it back from the battle to tell Duncan and the rest of his court what happened.
b) Macbeth has fought valiantly to put down the rebellion against Duncan.
c) The Thane of Ross comes with more news that one of Duncan's trusted noblemen, the Thane of Cawdor, has betrayed the King; even so, the King's forces were victorious.
d) The King decides to give the title *Thane of Cawdor* to Macbeth as a reward.

LINES TO LOOK OUT FOR

a) For brave Macbeth - well he deserves that name -

b) Till he unseamed him from the nave to th'chaps.

c) Assisted by that most disloyal traitor,
   The Thane of Cawdor,

d) What he hath lost, noble Macbeth hath won.

QUESTIONS

We have not seen Macbeth yet, but what impression do you have of him so far?

10

Scene 3

MACBETH AND BANQUO MEET THEIR FUTURE: IS IT GOOD NEWS OR BAD?

a) The witches meet again and mix up a charm.

b) Macbeth and Banquo are on their way home from the battle.

c) They come across the weird sisters.

d) The witches tell Macbeth that he'll be:
> Thane of Glamis (he already is)
> Thane of Cawdor (a better position with more power)
> King (best of all with total power).

e) Banquo's news is different; he is not going to be King but will be the father of Kings.

f) Macbeth is confused because he thinks the Thane of Cawdor is alive and well; he cannot even imagine being King.
The witches vanish.
Ross comes up and tells Macbeth that he's the new Thane of Cawdor. (The old one will be executed as a traitor.)
The witches have been proved right! Two out of three!

g) Macbeth is overwhelmed. Pleased for the present, but what about the future? There seems no way he could become King.

LINES TO LOOK OUT FOR

a) Peace! The charm's wound up.

b) So foul and fair* a day I have not seen. (* where have you heard this before?)

c) What are these
So withered, and so wild in their attire?

d) All hail, Macbeth, that shall be King hereafter!

e) Lesser than Macbeth, and greater.

f)   The Thane of Cawdor lives,
A prosperous gentleman: and to be King
Stands not within the prospect of belief,

g) This supernatural soliciting
Cannot be ill, cannot be good.

QUESTIONS

What in this scene could you describe as 'foul'?
What in this scene could you describe as 'fair'?

How do you think Macbeth feels at the end of this scene?

> *And oftentimes, to win us to our harm,*
> *The instruments of darkness tell us truths.*

Banquo says this after the witches have been proved right - what advice do you think he is trying to give Macbeth?

Can you work out what Banquo is saying at this moment.
What does Macbeth's expression suggest to you about his reaction to the witches?

Can you find a quotation to go with this picture?
Why is Macbeth looking directly at us?
In what way is this expression different from his expression in the first picture?

ACT 1

Scene 4

MACBETH'S REWARD

a) The Thane of Cawdor has been executed, although the King can hardly believe that he could have been a traitor.

b) The king thanks Macbeth and Banquo and promises to reward them generously.

c) The king announces that his son Malcolm will be the next king.

d) The king is going to spend time with Macbeth in his castle at Inverness.

e) It seems impossible now for Macbeth to become king - or is it?

LINES TO LOOK OUT FOR

a)   There's no art
To find the mind's construction in the face:-

b) More is thy due than more than all can pay.

c)   We will establish our estate upon
Our eldest, Malcolm.

d)   From hence to Inverness,
And bind us further to you.

e) *[aside]* The Prince of Cumberland! That is a step
On which I must fall down, or else o'er leap
For in my way it lies. Stars, hide your fires;
Let not light see my black and deep desires.

QUESTIONS

Most of the speeches in this scene are very formal, but Macbeth's speech at the end is completely different. Can you explain the difference in style?

Scene 5

LADY MACBETH IS QUICK TO FIND A WAY

a) Lady Macbeth reads a letter from her husband telling her what has happened.

b) She immediately sees how the prophecy could come true, if Macbeth were not so honest.

c) A messenger brings the news that the King is coming to stay the night, and Lady Macbeth realizes that this is her chance.

d) Macbeth arrives and she gives him a hint of what she has in mind.

LINES TO LOOK OUT FOR

a)   'Hail, King that shall be!' This
have I thought good to deliver thee . . .

b)   Yet I do fear thy nature;
It is too full o' th' milk of human kindness
To catch the nearest way.

c)   The raven himself is hoarse
That croaks the fatal entrance of Duncan
Under my battlements.

d)   He that's coming
Must be provided for.

QUESTIONS

Lady Macbeth immediately calls for help from evil spirits. Why does she need their help?

How much do you find out about the relationship between Macbeth and Lady Macbeth in this scene?

Shakespeare did not write in a crowning sequence like this. Can you explain why a director might add this and where it would come in the scene as written? How would you describe Macbeth's expression?

Can you suggest who will be the next person to speak and what they will say? Look back at Lady Macbeth's first speeches on hearing the news. Can you pick a line that would go with this picture?

Scene 6

WELCOME DUNCAN!

a) Duncan arrives at Macbeth's castle which seems very pleasant.

b) Lady Macbeth welcomes him warmly, and allows him to take her into the castle.

LINES TO LOOK OUT FOR

a) Where they most breed and haunt I have observed
The air is delicate.

b) See, see our honour'd hostess!

QUESTIONS

How does what you know about Macbeth and Lady Macbeth's plans affect the way you watch this scene?

Scene 7

THE PLAN IS FIXED!

a) Macbeth speaks his doubts to himself; he is especially upset because Duncan has been so good to him.

b) Lady Macbeth is furious that he is having doubts and puts the pressure on by accusing him of not being a man.

c) She finally convinces him that they can kill the king and explains how they will do it.

LINES TO LOOK OUT FOR

a)   .that but this blow
Might be the be-all and the end-all

b) And live a coward in thine own esteem,
Letting "I dare not" wait upon "I would".

When you durst do it, *then* you were a man;

c) I am settled, and bend up
Each corporal agent to this terrible feat.

QUESTIONS

What is troubling Macbeth's conscience at this stage?

How does Lady Macbeth put the pressure on? What do you think is the argument which finally convinces Macbeth?

*Work out three different captions for this picture.
The first describes the picture from the point of view of the King and his courtiers.
The second describes the picture from the point of view of Lady Macbeth's private thoughts.
The third should be based on Macbeth's thoughts at this moment.*

*What is happening in this picture?
Why is everyone smiling?*

*What is Lady Macbeth saying at this point?
How would you describe her expression?*

13

ACT 2

Scene 1

MACBETH CONVINCES HIMSELF

a) It is late. Banquo meets Macbeth and reminds him of the meeting with the weird sisters.

b) Macbeth, left on his own, imagines he sees a dagger, which seems to lead him on to do the deed.

LINES TO LOOK OUT FOR

a) I dreamt last night of the three weird sisters:
   To you they have showed some truth.

b)   There's no such thing.
   It is the bloody business which informs
   Thus to mine eyes.

c) I go, and it is done: the bell invites me.

QUESTIONS

Banquo cannot sleep. Can you explain why he is so uneasy?

After you have heard Macbeth's soliloquy (a speech delivered by the actor alone on stage), do you think that Macbeth will find it easy to murder Duncan?

If you were the director would you have Macbeth holding his own dagger for this scene?
If so can you find the line when he gets his dagger out?

Scene 2

THE MURDER:
LADY MACBETH TAKES OVER

a) Lady Macbeth has done her part in the murder and is waiting to hear whether Macbeth has done his.

b) Macbeth returns with blood on his hands. He is devastated and is already horrified by what he has done.

c) Lady Macbeth breaks into his ramblings with practical instructions. The daggers need to be returned and the blood must be washed off.

d) Macbeth is now incapable of any further action, so Lady Macbeth must return the daggers and smear the face of the grooms with blood.

e) They need to hurry because there is a knocking at the gate.

LINES TO LOOK OUT FOR

a)   Had he not resembled
    My father as he slept, I had done't.

b)   This is a sorry sight.

c)   Go get some water,
    And wash this filthy witness from your hand.

d)   I'll go no more.
    I am afraid to think what I have done;
    Look on't again I dare not.

QUESTIONS

Macbeth is a famous warrior and is used to killing people in battle. Why is he so frightened and distracted now?

Are there any small signs that Lady Macbeth, although appearing so cool, is troubled too?

We do not see the murder. Would it have been more horrifying if we could see the murder on stage? Would we have lost any of the horror that is in the scene as it is?

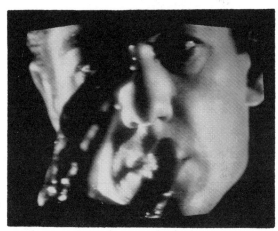

1.

2.

3.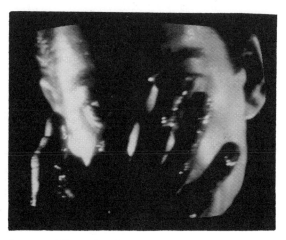

Can you find lines from this scene to go with each of these pictures?
Why did the television director decide to show a close up of Macbeth's hand in front of his face at this point?

ACT 2

Scene 3

DISCOVERY AND COVER UP

a) The porter, who has been drinking, takes his time opening the door, and rambles on about the devil and hell.

b) Macduff and Lennox have come to wake up the king. They meet Macbeth and tell him about the unnatural things that have been happening during the night.

c) Macduff returns having discovered the murder. The castle is in uproar.

d) Lady Macbeth appears, all innocent.

e) Macbeth slips away and kills the two grooms. Macduff is amazed as these are the key witnesses.

f) Lady Macbeth pretends to faint to avoid any more awkward questions.

g) Malcolm and Donalbain, the king's sons, decide that they will be safer away from Scotland.

LINES TO LOOK OUT FOR

a) *Lennox:* Goes the king hence today?
   Macbeth:　　　　　He does: he did appoint so

b) Lamentings heard i' th' air, strange screams of death . . .

c) *Macduff:*　　　Our royal master's murdered.
   Lady Macbeth:　What, in our house?

d) O, yet I do repent me of my fury
   That I did kill them.

e)　　　　　　　Where we are
   There's daggers in men's smiles.

QUESTIONS

Why do you think Shakespeare puts in a funny scene at this point in the play?

Why are we told about the strange events during the night?

Macbeth has to act as if he is shocked and appalled. How does he do this? Would you have been convinced by him?

Is Lady Macbeth any more believable?

How do you think the rest of the court will react to Malcolm and Donalbain running away?

Can you work out what is happening in the first picture? (The person with his back to you is Donalbain).
Can you suggest what is going through the minds of Banquo and MacDuff (in the background)?

Does Lady Macbeth look as if she is overdoing it?

Scene 4

MACBETH IN THE CLEAR?

a) An old man tells Ross of more dreadful happenings during that night.

b) Macduff comes in and we learn that Macbeth has already gone to Scone to be crowned. All is going well for Macbeth especially as suspicion has fallen on the king's sons.

LINES TO LOOK OUT FOR

a)   'Tis unnatural,
Even like the deed that's done.

b) Malcolm and Donalbain, the King's two sons
Are stol'n away and fled; which puts upon them
Suspicion of the deed.

QUESTIONS

If you were Shakespeare and you had got this far, how would you continue the play?

Would it be a good play if it ended here?

ACT 3

Scene 1

MACBETH PLANS A MURDER

a) Banquo is suspicious, but remembers that his offspring will be kings.
b) Macbeth, with all his royal followers, asks after Banquo and is concerned to find out what he will be doing that evening. There is to be a big feast.
c) On his own again, Macbeth talks about his fears of Banquo.
d) Macbeth bullies and persuades his two henchmen to murder Banquo *and* his son Fleance.

LINES TO LOOK OUT FOR

a)   . . . and I fear
   Thou playd'st most foully for 't.

b) Ride you this afternoon? . . .
   Is't far you ride? . . .
   Goes Fleance with you? . . .

c) To be thus is nothing, but to be safely thus -
   Our fears in Banquo stick deep.

d)   Both of you
   Know Banquo was your enemy.

                . . . and with him -
   To leave no rubs nor botches in the work -
   Fleance his son . . .

QUESTIONS

How can you tell from the way he behaves in the first part of this scene that Macbeth is now king? How is he acting the part?

Why is he so concerned to have Fleance killed?

What tactics does he use to persuade his henchmen to murder Banquo?

Scene 2

MACBETH STARTS TO SHOW THE STRAIN

a) Macbeth tells Lady Macbeth about his uneasiness and his terrible dreams.
b) Lady Macbeth tries to reassure him.
c) Macbeth tells her of his worry about Banquo, but does not reveal his plan to murder him and his son.

LINES TO LOOK OUT FOR

a) We have scotch'd the snake, not kill'd it.

   In the affliction of these terrible dreams
   That shake us nightly.

b) Gentle my lord, sleek o er your rugged look,
   Be bright and jovial among your guests tonight

c) Be innocent of the knowledge, dearest chuck

QUESTIONS

Do you understand why Macbeth is feeling so uneasy now that he is king?

Why does he not tell Lady Macbeth about his plans for Banquo?

Can you remember any other mention of sleep and bad dreams in the play so far?

Compare this picture of the King and his court with the picture of King Duncan and his court on page 13. How would you describe the atmosphere at this moment?

Why has the director positioned Macbeth in the low foreground and Lady Macbeth higher in the background?
Does this picture tell you anything about their relationship at this stage in the play?

Scene 3

MURDER IN THE DARK

a) The two murderers wait outside the castle for Banquo to return. They are joined by a mysterious third murderer.

b) Banquo and Fleance lead their horses up. The murderers attack and the light gives out. Banquo is killed, but Fleance gets away.

c) The murderers hurry back to Macbeth.

LINES TO LOOK OUT FOR

a) But who did bid thee join with us?

b)   Fly, good Fleance, fly, fly, fly!
   Thou mayst revenge.

c) We have lost best half of our affair.

QUESTIONS

Why do you think Shakespeare brought in the third murderer?

Why did Shakespeare have the light falling and going out?

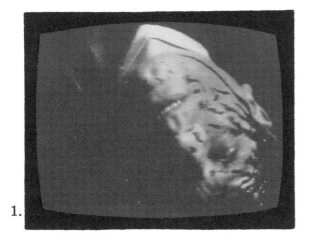

1.

2.

3.

4.

Put these four pictures in the right order.
Choose a line from the scene to go with each picture.

ACT 3
Scene 4

MACBETH'S MAD VISION RUINS THE BANQUET

a) Macbeth acts out his part as host as his guests take their places.

b) The murderer comes in and reports on Banquo's death and Fleance's escape.

c) Macbeth is disturbed, but is drawn back to the table by Lady Macbeth.

d) Macbeth can find no seat; instead he sees only the bloody figure of Banquo. He is horrified. The rest are baffled. Lady Macbeth tries to cover up.

e) The 'ghost' returns to Macbeth twice; each time he is more upset. The guests are persuaded by Lady Macbeth that he is ill.

f) After the final appearance, Lady Macbeth ends the meal and the guests leave.

g) Calm again. Macbeth decides to go back to the three witches; he needs to know what is to happen to him.

LINES TO LOOK OUT FOR

a) Ourself will mingle with society
   And play the humble host.

b) There the grown serpent lies; the worm that's fled
   Hath nature that in time will venom breed.

c) Thou canst not say I did it. Never shake
   Thy gory locks at me.

   - This is the very painting of your fear;

   The time has been
   - That, when the brains were out, the man would die
   And there an end.

d) I pray you speak not; he grows worse and worse.

e)   I will tomorrow,
   And betimes I will, to the weird sisters;
   More shall they speak.

                    I am in blood
   Stepped in so far that, should I wade no more,
   Returning were as tedious as go o'er.

QUESTIONS

Why do you think this banquet is so important to Macbeth and Lady Macbeth?

Why do you think Shakespeare decided to haunt Macbeth with the ghost of Banquo rather than with the ghost of Duncan?

How does Lady Macbeth react to   Macbeth?
                                    the rest of the guests?

What does this scene tell us about Macbeth's state of mind at this part in the play?

This is Macbeth and Lady Macbeth at the start of the banquet. What do you think he is saying?
What do you think he is thinking?
What does Lady Macbeth's expression tell you about her feelings?

This is Lady Macbeth at the end of the banquet scene. Why is she so distressed?
Can you find a line to go with this moment?

Scene 5

Although this scene appears in most copies of the play, nobody is quite sure why it is there. Many people do not think that Shakespeare even wrote it, and it is usually left out of productions. The only interest might be to look at Hecate's speech and compare it with another piece of genuine Shakespeare at his best. The difference is striking.

Scene 6

THE FIGHT BACK BEGINS

a) Without saying so directly, Lennox tells another Lord about his suspicions. He hears that Malcolm has gone to England to ask the English King to send soldiers to remove Macbeth. Macduff has also gone to England.

b) Macbeth is preparing for war.

LINES TO LOOK OUT FOR

a) And the right-valiant Banquo walk'd too late;
Whom, you may say, if't please you, Fleance kill'd,
For Fleance fled. Men must not walk too late.

b)   And this report
Hath so exasperate the King that he
Prepares for some attempt of war.

QUESTIONS

Why is Lennox so careful in the way he describes what has happened?

What do you think the director said to these two actors about the way to act this scene?

ACT 4

Scene 1

MORE PROMISES FROM THE WEIRD SISTERS

a) The weird sisters mix up a horrible brew to help with the magic spell. Macbeth arrives and demands to know what the future holds.

b) He is told three things: to beware MacDuff; that he cannot be killed by any man born naturally from a woman; that he will not be killed until the forest of Burnham moves to his castle at Dunsinane.

c) He then asks if Banquo's descendants will indeed be Kings, and the answer comes in the form of eight ghostly Kings of which the last is Banquo.

d) The witches vanish, and Lennox enters bringing the news that Macduff has fled to England. Macbeth decides to kill Macduff's wife and entire family.

LINES TO LOOK OUT FOR

a) Cool it with a baboon's blood,
   Then the charm is firm and good.

b) Macbeth shall never vanquished be until
   Great Birnam Wood to high Dunsinane Hill
   Shall come against him.
   Macbeth: That will never be.

c) Horrible sight! Now I see 'tis true;
   For the blood-boltered Banquo smiles upon me,
   And points at them for his.

d)   No boasting like a fool;
   This deed I'll do before this purpose cool:

QUESTIONS

What do you think Macbeth expects to hear from the witches? In what ways is Macbeth encouraged by what he hears?

What causes him to be fearful?

How does Lennox's news fit in with the witches' predictions?

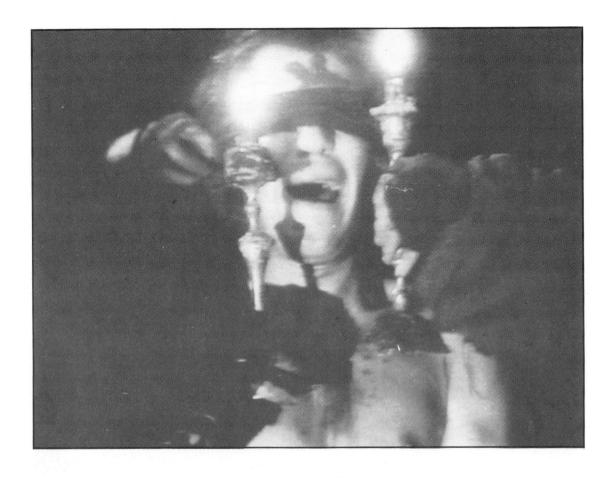

Macbeth is being shown the descendents of Banquo.
Why do you think Macbeth has been blindfolded for this part of the scene?
Why has the director given the witches candles? What effect as they have on the audience? What do they suggest to you?

Scene 2

MACDUFF'S FAMILY MURDERED

a) Lady Macduff complains to Ross that her husband has left her. She thinks he is frightened, and doesn't know that he plans to bring an army.

b) Lady Macduff's talk with her small son is interrupted by a messenger telling them to flee from the murderers who are approaching.

c) Before she can take any action they arrive and kill her and her son.

LINES TO LOOK OUT FOR

a)   You know not
Whether it was his wisdom or his fear.

b) Was my father a traitor, mother?

             Whither should I fly?
I have done no harm.

QUESTIONS

We have not met Lady Macduff before and yet we are horrified by her death. How much do we know about her by the time she dies? What makes the murder so horrible?

Scene 3

GOOD NEWS AND BAD NEWS IN ENGLAND

a) Prince Malcolm tells Macduff that he, Malcolm, will be a wicked king, even worse than Macbeth. Macduff curses him, and then Malcolm reveals that he was only testing Macduff's honesty and reliability, in case Macduff was a spy from Macbeth.

b) Malcolm and Macduff hear that Edward, the English King, is such a virtuous king that he is able to cure sick people simply by touching them.

c) Ross brings the terrible news that Macduff's wife and children have been murdered. At first Macduff can hardly believe it; then he swears vengeance against Macbeth.

LINES TO LOOK OUT FOR

a) If such a one be fit to govern, speak:
I am as I have spoken.
   Macduff: Fit to govern!
     No, not to live!

b) And sundry blessings hang about his throne
That speak him full of grace.

c) Did you say all? O hell-kite! All?
What, all my pretty chickens and their dam
At one fell swoop?

QUESTIONS

Why do you think Shakespeare gives so much time to a scene in which the qualities of good and bad kings are discussed?

How does Shakespeare make us *feel* Macduff's shock at hearing the news of his family's murder?

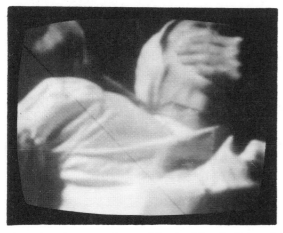

Why has the director dressed Lady Macduff in white for this scene?
What is the difference between the way this murder takes place and the way the murder of Banquo takes place?

Malcolm is speaking. What do you think he is saying to Macduff?

ACT 5
Scene 1

LADY MACBETH SLEEPWALKS

a) In Macbeth's castle at Dunsinane, Lady Macbeth's serving-woman has called a doctor because Lady Macbeth is behaving strangely.

b) Together they see Lady Macbeth walking in her sleep, and saying things aloud to herself which make no sense to them.

LINES TO LOOK OUT FOR

a) It is an accustomed action with her, to seem thus washing her hands:

b) Yet who would have thought the old man to have had so much blood in him?

I tell you yet again, Banquo's buried. He cannot come out on's grave.

QUESTIONS

Which of Lady Macbeth's strange words and actions do *you* understand, even though the doctor and the gentlewoman do not?

How does Lady Macbeth compare now with the way she was when we last saw her, at the feast where Macbeth saw Banquo's ghost?

1.

2.

3.

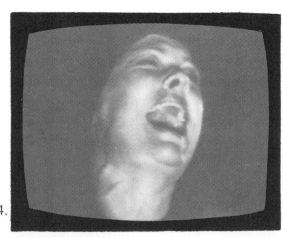

4.

*Can you find a line to go with each of these pictures?
If you had to pick one picture which summed up Lady Macbeth's state of mind at this point in the play which would you choose?*

Scene 2

SCOTTISH REBELS JOIN WITH ENGLISH ARMY

a) Scots lords who are opposed to Macbeth are taking their soldiers to join Malcolm, Macduff and the English army in Birnam Wood, near Dunsinane Castle.

b) They discuss the rumours that Macbeth is preparing to fight, that he has gone mad, and that his soldiers are leaving him.

LINES TO LOOK OUT FOR

Now does he feel
His secret murders sticking on his hands;
. . . Now does he feel his title
Hang loose about him, like a giant's robe
Upon a dwarfish thief.

QUESTIONS

Why do we prick up our ears when the lords say that they will meet the English in Birnam Wood?

Scene 3

MACBETH PREPARES TO FIGHT

a) Macbeth still trusts in the promises the weird sisters gave him, and begins to put on his armour while rushing about giving orders.

b) The doctor tells him that his wife is very ill in her mind, and that he does not know the cure.

LINES TO LOOK OUT FOR

a) And that which should accompany old age,
As honour, love, obedience, troops of friends,
I must not look to have; but in their stead,
Curses not loud, but deep . . .

b) Canst thou not minister to a mind diseas'd?
Doctor: Therein the patient
Must minister to himself.

QUESTIONS

Not everything Macbeth says in this scene is brave and defiant. What else is running through his mind?

Why can't the doctor help Lady Macbeth?

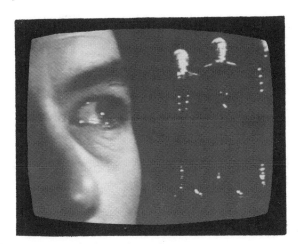

This is a special effect for television: the eye of Macbeth and the Scottish lords.
Why did the director choose to compose this shot in this way? What effect did he hope it would have on the audience?

In this shot, Macbeth is crouching in front of the King's robes. What message do you think the director is trying to get across?

ACT 5

Scene 4

ENGLISH AND SCOTS COMBINE FORCES

a) All the forces opposed to Macbeth meet in Birnam Wood.
b) Each soldier cuts a branch from a tree to hold in front of him, to prevent Macbeth realising how many troops are against him.
c) They have heard that Macbeth will stay inside his castle.

LINES TO LOOK OUT FOR

Let every soldier hew him down a bough
And bear't before him:

QUESTIONS

From the evidence you have heard in this scene and the impression you had of Macbeth's castle in the one before, which side is most likely to win the battle? Why?

Scene 5

TWO SHOCKS FOR MACBETH

a) Macbeth is still full of confidence, until two things happen to shake him -
b) Lady Macbeth dies, and
c) A messenger reports that Birnam Wood is coming towards the castle.

LINES TO LOOK OUT FOR

a)   Our castle's strength
   Will laugh a siege to scorn.

b)   Out, out, brief candle!
   Life's but a walking shadow, a poor player
   That struts and frets his hour upon the stage,
   And then is heard no more.

c) I pull in resolution, and begin
   To doubt th'equivocation of the fiend
   That lies like truth.

QUESTIONS

How does Macbeth take the news of his wife's death (perhaps even suicide)?

How does he take the news about the moving wood?

Why has the director included the doll used by the witches to predict Macbeth's future?
Compare this with the picture for scene 2.

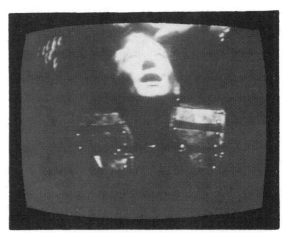

Can you find the lines that go with this picture?
Is this a more sympathetic view of Macbeth?

Scene 6

THE BATTLE BEGINS

Malcolm orders Siward into the first attack; he himself and Macduff have a different job (to find Macbeth).

Scene 7

THE BATTLE

a) Macbeth has come out of his castle. He meets and kills Siward's son, confident that no man born of woman can kill him.
b) Macduff is looking only for Macbeth.
c) The castle has been surrendered, as most of Macbeth's men do not want to fight. Malcolm goes to enter it.

LINES TO LOOK OUT FOR

a)   What's he
   That was not born of woman? Such a one
   Am I to fear, or none.

b)   Tyrant, show thy face!
   If thou beest slain and with no stroke of mine,
   My wife and children's ghosts will haunt me still.

QUESTIONS

How does Shakespeare, using only a few actors and a small stage, convey the idea of a battle with lots of soldiers?

Scene 8

VICTORY AND THE WITCHES' FINAL TRICK

a) Macduff meets Macbeth, and Macbeth learns to his horror that Macduff was not born naturally, but taken out of his mother's womb prematurely by an operation. They fight.
b) Siward learns that his son is dead, but that his troops have been completely successful.
c) Macduff arrives with Macbeth's head, and Malcolm is greeted as the new and rightful King of Scotland.

LINES TO LOOK OUT FOR

a) And be these juggling fiends no more believ'd
   That palter with us in a double sense.

b) Though Birnam Wood be come to Dunsinane,
   And thou oppos'd, being of no woman born,
   Yet I will try the last.

c) Hail, King! for so thou art. Behold where stands
   Th'usurper's cursed head. The time is free.

QUESTIONS

How does Macbeth behave when he realises the witches have tricked him fatally?

Old Siward is glad his son died fighting bravely. Who else was praised as a good soldier earlier in the play?

Malcolm calls Macbeth and Lady Macbeth "this dead butcher and his fiend-like queen". Do you agree with his description?

Can you find lines to go with each of these pictures?

"THE TIME IS FREE"

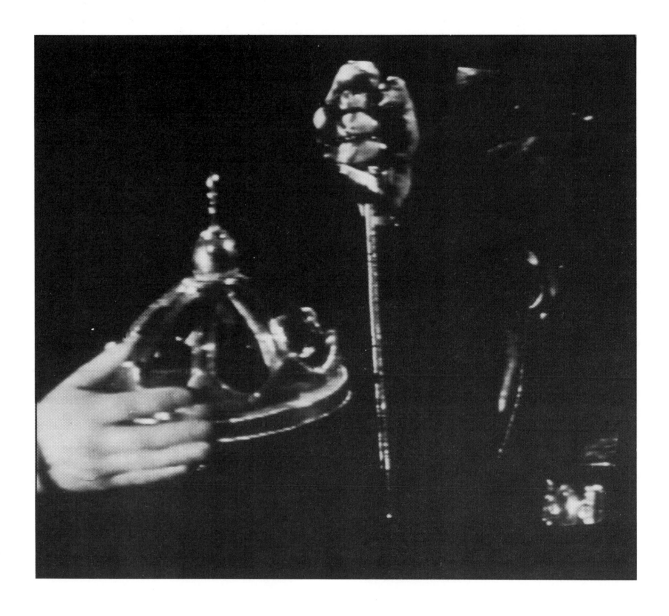

This is the last image of the television version of the Royal Shakespeare Company's production of Macbeth. Can you explain why the director used this shot to finish the play?

WRITING ABOUT MACBETH

In this section are suggestions for work on *Macbeth* aimed at increasing your understanding of the play. All of them involve discussing aspects of the play in groups, and many of them have suggestions for writing that could be included in a Literature folder.

PUBLIC . . .

LOOK LIKE THE INNOCENT FLOWER -
BUT BE THE SERPENT UNDER IT . . . *(I.5.64)*

This is Lady Macbeth's advice to Macbeth as they prepare to welcome King Duncan to their castle. Already the king has been deceived by someone he trusted, and he has observed that a person's *public* face does not necessarily reveal their *private* thoughts.

> There's no art
> To find the mind's construction in the face:
> He was a gentleman on whom I built
> An absolute trust.
> *(I.4.12)*

This idea that 'things are not what they seem' re-appears again and again in *Macbeth*:

— The witches' prophecy *seems* to be good but is really bad.
— Macbeth's castle *seems* to be safe but is really a place of murder.
— What *seems* to be a wood is really an army.

Of course once the plan to murder Duncan takes root, Macbeth and Lady Macbeth have to live the rest of their lives with a public face of innocence and a private feeling of guilt.

Here are some quotations from the play which express the difference between the public face (what seems to be) and the private thoughts (what really is):

> False face must hide what the false heart doth know *(1.7.83)*
>
> To show an unfelt sorrow is an office
> Which the false man does easy. *(2.3.138)*
>
> . . . but wail his fall
> Who I myself struck down. *(3.1.122)*
>
> Gentle my lord, sleek o'er your rugged looks,
> Be bright and jovial among your guests tonight. *(3.2.28)*
>
> And make our faces vizards to our hearts
> Disguising what they are. *(3.2.34)*

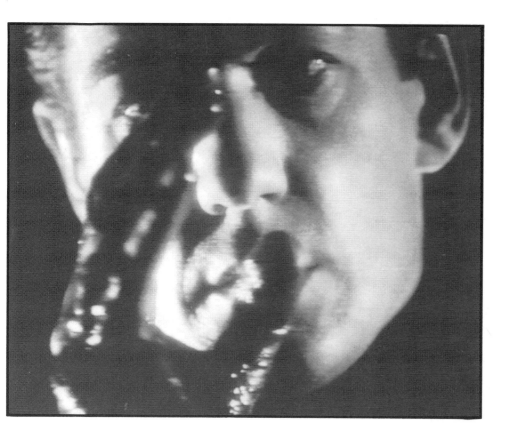

WHAT TO DO

Write a story in which the main character has to:
'Look like the innocent flower, but be the serpent under it'.
It does not have to be a modern version of *Macbeth*, but you could make the story more interesting by relating it to the play.

a) You could use the quotations above as chapter or section headings. For example, the first section, in which the villain meets the victim and has to act innocent, could have the title:
False face must hide what the false heart doth know.

b) You could base your story on the same structure as the play *Macbeth*:
1. THE FALSE WELCOME
2. THE TREACHEROUS DEED
3. FAKE GRIEF
4. ACTING THE INNOCENT

Some suggestions:
— the star player on the school team
an accident is arranged by the person who has been kept out of the team . . .
— the well respected leader of the gang (or oil company?)
a nasty accident is arranged by the person next in line for leadership . . .

PERSUASION

Lady Macbeth has to persuade Macbeth to murder
the King and so make the weird sisters' prophecy come
true.

Can you remember how she does it? Here are some
example of her tactics (from *1.7.35-61*):

> *Flattery;*
> > Great Glamis! Worthy Cawdor!
> Greater than both, by the all-hail hereafter.

> *Accusing him of cowardice;*
> And live a coward in thine own esteem
> Letting "I dare not" wait upon "I would".

> *Questioning his manhood;*
> When you durst do it, then you were a man.

> *Reassuring;*
> But screw your courage to the sticking point,
> And we'll not fail.

WHAT TO DO

Write a scene from a play in which one person is
persuading another person to do something wrong,
for example:

— to commit a murder to gain the insurance money.
— to break into a shop.
— to cheat in an exam.

This second person had agreed to go along with the
idea but has decided to change his or her mind. Their
first speech could be a modern version of Macbeth's
"We will proceed no further with this business".

Try to use all four of the tactics used by Lady Macbeth.
Do not worry too much about explaining the story;
concentrate on making the persuasion as powerful as
possible.

GUILT

A LITTLE WATER CLEARS US OF THIS DEED
(2.3.66)

Lady Macbeth is trying to convince Macbeth that all will be well after they have murdered Duncan. The rest of the play shows us how wrong she is. Already Macbeth is feeling guilty; his conscience is beginning to work on him. He may be King, but is he safe? Will he be able to live with himself? He is not only guilty, but afraid.

Several things happen to show us how this guilt and fear affect him:

— He fears Banquo and has him killed.
— He is deeply disturbed at the banquet and 'sees' the ghost of Banquo.
— He cannot sleep, and when he does is afflicted by terrible dreams.
— He can trust no one; he must murder more and more people in order to feel safe.
— He goes back to the witches desperate for more information.

WHAT TO DO

Write a story in which guilt and fear work on someone who has committed a crime. Try to include in your story some of the things which happen to Macbeth.

— Has trouble sleeping; suffers from terrible nightmares.
— Has to commit more crimes to cover his/her tracks.
— Begins to see things.
— Desperately needs reassurance.

You could write this story from the point of view of the guilty person. The story could be in the form of his/her diary or even just that person's thoughts.

PREDICTIONS

1. All hail Macbeth! Hail to thee, Thane of Cawdor!
2. All hail Macbeth, that shalt be King hereafter.
   (1.3)
3. Macbeth! Beware MacDuff.
4.   Laugh to scorn
   The power of man, for none of woman born
   Shall harm Macbeth.
5. Macbeth shall never vanquished be until
   Great Burnam wood to high Dunsinane Hill
   Shall come against him.
   (4.1)

The weird sisters make five different predictions to Macbeth. All of them come true.
Banquo is wary of predictions because he believes that the 'instruments of darkness' tell truths in order to 'betray us in deepest consequence'.
A prediction may appear to be a happy one, but the final consequences may be far from happy.

WHAT TO DO

Write a story in which the main character receives several predictions which sound good, but in fact turn out to be very harmful.

The story could begin like this:

It sounded too good to be true when the old fortune teller at the fair made her prediction. Now I wish I had never gone near the tent. She had looked at my hand and said . . .

HOROSCOPES

☆ **CANCER** (June 21-July 20). You may have to consider the feelings of another person and discover they have been more unsettled than you realised.

☆ **PISCES** (Feb. 19-March 20). There may be confusion over a family matter.

☆ **CAPRICORN** (Dec. 21-Jan. 19): Expect the unexpected and you won't be let down.

☆ **TAURUS** (April 21-May 20). Something that happened last month could now influence your life.

☆ **ARIES** (March 21-April 20). A busy time for you these days doing unusual and exciting things. You could be talking to a nurse or other medical people on behalf of someone else.

☆ **VIRGO** (Aug. 22-Sept. 22). A chain of events will alter your life considerably.

☆ **SCORPIO** (Oct. 23-Nov. 22): Your true capabilities will soon be realised. Your emotional life is steadier these days with less tension.

☆ **GEMINI** (May 21-June 20). A new start or job seems likely.

☆ **LEO** (July 21-Aug. 21). Don't get involved with someone who would number you with their problems.

☆ **AQUARIUS** (Jan. 20-Feb. 18). Things happen rather suddenly. You may have to dash off at a moment's notice.

☆ **LIBRA** (Sept. 23-Oct. 22): You sometimes wonder whether you should have followed a completely different career.

☆ **SAGITTARIUS** (Nov. 23-Dec. 20): Some of you could be getting promotion or receiving some praise for hard work.

WHAT TO DO

These horoscopes were taken from the Daily Mirror on 3rd July 1979.

BUT: many of them could apply to the characters in *Macbeth*.

* Try to find a character to go with each horoscope and show the horoscope could be said to come true in the play.

* Based on the witches' predictions and your knowledge of what happens in the play prepare a horoscope for:

i)   Macbeth
ii) Banquo
iii) Lady Macbeth
iv) Lady Macduff
v)   Malcolm
vi) Duncan

Pick at least two of these.

Before you begin look at the style in which the horoscopes at the top of the page and the ones in your newspaper or magazines are written. They are never *too* definite, so Duncan would not have: 'You will be killed tomorrow'; it is more likely to be 'expect a very sudden change in your life'.

A TRIAL

THE TRIAL OF MACBETH AND LADY MACBETH

Suppose that Macbeth and Lady Macbeth were arrested after the murder of Duncan. When the case comes to court, Macbeth pleads guilty to the murder, but Lady Macbeth pleads not guilty.

Two lawyers are needed. One, a defence lawyer, will try to get Macbeth a lighter sentence by showing that, although he did the murder, there are things to be said in his favour. The other, a prosecuting lawyer, will try to show that Lady Macbeth deserves a heavy sentence, even though she did not actually kill the King.

WHAT TO DO

(Work in pairs)

1. Decide whether you will defend Macbeth or prosecute Lady Macbeth.

2. Working from memory, find all the arguments you can to support your case. You will need to consider questions like these:

MACBETH
a) What kind of man was he before the murder? (Did he have a good reputation?)
b) Did anybody put strong pressure on him, and if so, how?
c) Was he in his right mind? (Any strange experiences, hallucinations, etc.?)
d) Did he find it easy to murder Duncan?
e) Did he regret killing Duncan? (Any signs of remorse, or disgust with himself?)

LADY MACBETH
a) Did she suggest murder to her husband?
b) Did she encourage him to do it?
c) Did she put pressure on him to do it?
d) Did she help plan it?
e) Did she help carry it out?
f) Did she try to cover it up?
g) What did she feel about it afterwards?

3. Look back at the play (up to the end of Act 2, Scene 2) and find things that Macbeth or Lady Macbeth actually said, which you quote to prove your points, e.g.:

a) Duncan calls Macbeth "Valiant cousin! Worthy gentleman!" and promises to make him Thane of Cawdor.

The captain, speaking of the battle, says:

"Brave Macbeth - well he deserves that name."
(Act 1, Scene 2)

b) When Macbeth says that the King is coming to stay with them that night and leaving the next day, Lady Macbeth says:

"O never
Shall sun that morrow see!"

Later, speaking of murder, she says:

"Leave all the rest to me." (Act 1, Scene 5)

"My client, Macbeth, admits that he murdered King Duncan, but I shall show the court that the case is not as simple as that . . ."

4. Using your notes, write out your speech to the court. Remember that as a lawyer you are allowed to skip over awkward points and just concentrate on the points that suit your case.

MACBETH ON THE STAGE

As you work through *Macbeth* for your exam it would be easy to forget that this play was written to be performed on stage.

The person who decides how a play is presented on stage is called the DIRECTOR. He or she will read the play very carefully indeed and decide how each scene is going to work on stage. A director will expect the actors to have their own ideas, but he or she will need to have a picture of the whole play.

For each scene of the play a director needs to ask several questions, of which the most important one is:

1. How can I make the audience experience this scene in the way I want them to? (By getting them gripped, laughing, crying, horrified, etc.)

The other questions are:

2. What objects will I have on stage for this scene and where will they be placed?

3. Where will the actors come on to the stage from? Where will they move to, and when? (Actors will be given some freedom in this, but the director must have an overall plan.)

4. How will the actors behave during this scene? What are they supposed to be feeling? How will they show these feelings in the way they move and the way they speak their lines?

5. What will the actors who are not speaking be doing in the background?

6. What will the lighting be like? Will there be any extra sounds? (Music, sound effects, etc.)

Before the director begins rehearsals he/she must visualize the scene in his/her mind's eye and then write notes, usually on a copy of the script. These notes will remind the director of the answers to the questions.

On the next page you will find a page taken from a director's script. You can see she has made notes on the script.

MACBETH ON THE STAGE

What about stockings over their heads? They must look threatening and cool to begin with.

Very dim lighting — with shadows on the back wall (perhaps dark clouds?)

Scene III.   [*Near the palace.*]

Enter Three Murderers.

First and second come in from E③ ahead. 3rd is stalking behind.

Spoken over his shoulder as he enters

First Murderer. But who did bid thee join with us?

Third Murderer.   Macbeth.

This surprises the other two — they both stop.

Second Murderer. He needs not our mistrust; since he delivers
Our offices and what we have to do
To the direction just.°

Stops in mid movement

⊗

We must feel that they are dealing with their suspicions.

First Murderer.   Then stand with us.
The west yet glimmers with some streaks of day.   5
Now spurs the lated° traveler apace
To gain the timely inn, and near approaches
The subject of our watch.

Third Murderer.   Hark! I hear horses.

Moves up onto dais.

Moves into darkness of E⑧.

Banquo. (*Within*) Give us a light there, ho!

Second Murderer.   Then 'tis he. The rest
~~That are within the note of expectation°~~   10
~~Already are i' th' court.~~

Crouches below dais.

First Murderer.   His horses go about.

flattens himself against back wall.

Third Murderer. Almost a mile: but he does usually—
So all men do—from hence to th' palace gate
Make it their walk.

from Ent. A. with bright, single light.

Enter Banquo and Fleance, with a torch.

Second Murderer. A light, a light!

Third Murderer.   'Tis he.

1st M follows them round and silently moves onto dais.

First Murderer.   Stand to 't.   15

at Z.

Banquo. It will be rain tonight.

First Murderer.   Let it come down.

jumps down

LIGHTS DOWN

[*They set upon Banquo.*]

Banquo. O, treachery! Fly, good Fleance, fly, fly, fly!

[*Exit Fleance.*]

tries Ex B, then makes it back to Ex A.

Moves centre stage — and B. thrashes about with 3 murderers flaying about — B killed dropped over dais. Q

Thou mayst revenge. O slave! [*Dies.*]

Third Murderer. Who did strike out the light?

First Murderer.   Was 't not the way?°

Third Murderer. There's but one down; the son is fled.   20

Second Murderer. We have lost best half of our affair.

sits down on the dais exhausted.

First Murderer. Well, let's away and say how much is done.   *Exeunt.*

MACBETH ON THE STAGE

Here is a plan of the theatre:

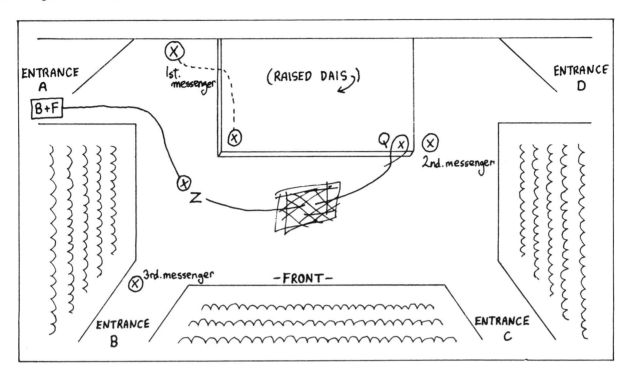

WHAT TO DO

Here is a list of three scenes in *Macbeth* which a director would need to think about carefully:

ACT II Scene 3. Lines 51 to 125.
The discovery of Duncan's murder and Macbeth and Lady Macbeth's cover-up.

ACT III Scene 4.
The banquet scene in which Macbeth 'sees' the ghost of Banquo. (N.B. an important decision is whether or not to have Banquo's 'ghost' on stage.)

ACT V Scene 1.
The sleep-walking scene.

1. Ask your teacher to photocopy the scene you are interested in directing.
2. Stick your copy of the scene onto a larger sheet of paper so that you have plenty of room to scribble notes.
3. Go through the six questions and decide how you will present the play.
4. You can *either* use the plan of the theatre on this page *or* do a plan of the theatre space in your own school.
5. You will need to include sketches and diagrams to explain the more complicated bits.

Obviously the best way to see how successful you have been as a director is to TRY IT OUT with a group of people in a space. If your ideas work, you might want to go on and put the scene on in front of an audience.

INTERVIEWING THE CHARACTERS

Suppose you had the opportunity to interview some
of the characters in *Macbeth*.
Which character would you choose to interview?
What questions would you ask him or her?

Here is part of an interview with Banquo:

Interviewer: Tell me, Banquo, what was your reaction to the witches? Were you scared of them?

Banquo: Not really. I have seen many strange things in my time, and I don't pretend to understand everything. As I said to Macbeth at the time,
"The earth hath bubbles, as the water has,
And these are of them."
I was more fascinated than frightened. You must remember that we were on our way back from the battle. I was exhausted. I couldn't make them out, but I was suspicious.

Interviewer: And what about Macbeth? How do you think he reacted?

Banquo: He was very jumpy from the start. When they made their prophecies, I was surprised to see him become very upset, because all the predictions favoured him.

Interviewer: Why was he upset?

Banquo: I'm not sure. We'd both been given some good news, even if it was conflicting. Then when one of the prophecies came true almost immediately, I was a bit shaken . . .

WHAT TO DO

Here is a list of characters it might be interesting to
interview:

Macbeth: You could interview Macbeth at different
times during the play or interview him just before
the battle and ask him about whether he has any
regrets.

Lady Macbeth: Ask her about how she planned the
murder, and what were the problems. Ask her about
her impression of Macbeth before the murder of
Duncan, and then after.

Banquo: Get him to talk about his suspicions of
Macbeth.

The Doctor: What was life like in the castle in the
later stages? How did he feel after he had seen Lady
Macbeth sleep walk?

When you write your interview try to include lines
from the play (look back at the example interview
with Banquo for some ideas).

'MACBETH'

The Plot

Macbeth and Banquo meet three witches who tell Macbeth that he will become King of Scotland. They tell Banquo that his children will become kings.

Macbeth tells his wife about his meeting with the witches. She decides they should kill King Duncan as soon as possible so that Macbeth will become king. She finally persuades her husband to commit the murder.

Macduff discovers Duncan's body and is horrified.

Duncan's sons, Malcolm and Donalbain, run away because they are afraid that they may be murdered too. Malcolm goes to England.

Macbeth is crowned king.

Macbeth does not want Banquo's children to become kings after him as the witches have promised so he arranges for Banquo and his son, Fleance to be murdered. Banquo is killed but Fleance escapes.

Macbeth meets the witches again to find out more about his future. They tell him to beware of Macduff but also tell him that he cannot be killed by any man born naturally. Macbeth now feels safe.

Macduff goes to England to join Malcolm who is raising an army to fight against Macbeth.

Macbeth is annoyed that Macduff has gone to join Malcolm so in order to get his revenge, he orders the murder of Lady Macduff and her children.

Gradually, Macbeth's lords leave him to join Malcolm because they realise he is not a good king.

Lady Macbeth eventually kills herself because she begins to feel guilty about what they have done and goes mad.

Malcolm and his army face Macbeth in battle.

Macduff, who was not born naturally because his mother died in childbirth, kills Macbeth.

Malcolm is made King of Scotland.

macbeth/mp

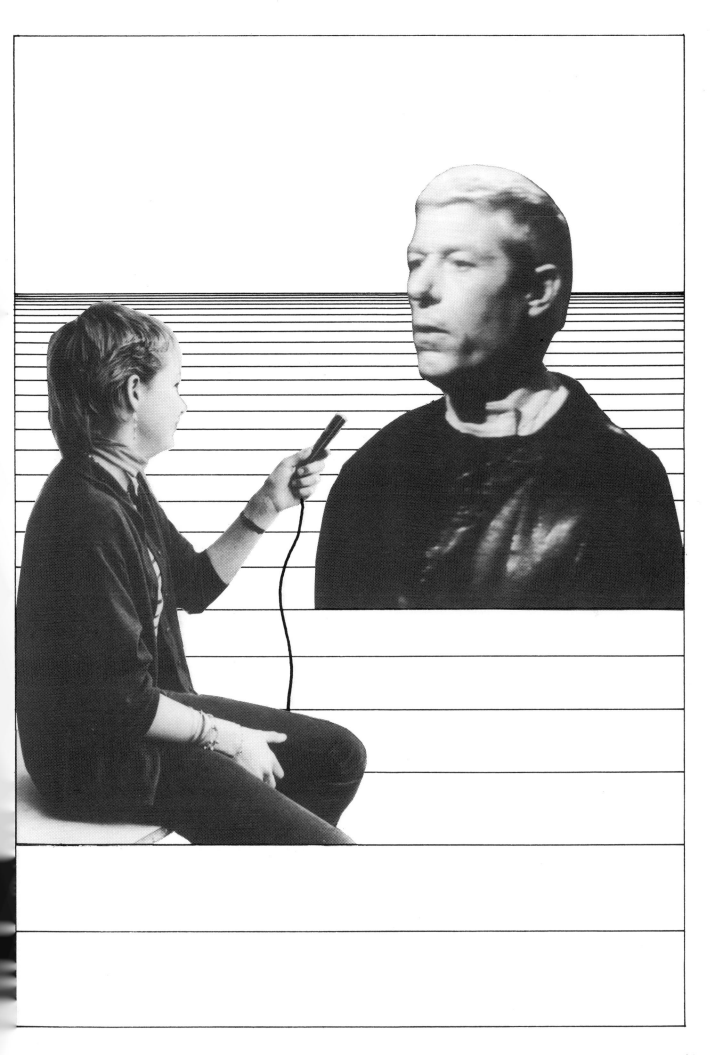

MACBETH: HERO OR VILLAIN?

"This tyrant, whose sole name blisters our tongues,
Was once thought honest."

"O valiant cousin! Worthy gentleman!"

"this dead butcher"

To help you write an essay about Macbeth, which explores his role in the play:

1. Discuss with someone whether each of these statements is true:

   a) Macbeth is a brave and loyal soldier.

   b) Macbeth is a fool to believe what the witches say.

   c) Macbeth is weak compared to Lady Macbeth.

   d) Macbeth regrets killing Duncan.

   e) Although Banquo's ghost terrifies him, Macbeth doesn't regret killing Banquo.

   f) Macbeth rules Scotland by murder and terror.

   g) Macbeth admits to himself he is evil, so he is honest, and not a hypocrite.

   h) Macbeth never loses his bravery, even when he realises the witches have tricked him.

APPEARANCE AND REALITY

Macbeth is full of things that are not what they seem to be, and people whose *reality* is different from their *appearance*.

Here are some examples:

1. The weird sisters look like men *and* women. (1,3,46)

2. It's not certain at first whether they really exist, or are just visions. (1,3,82)

3. Macbeth and Lady Macbeth seem to Duncan to be loyal, loving and trustworthy, when he enters their castle.

4. Banquo describes the castle where Duncan is to die as a pleasant and healthy place.

5. Macbeth and Lady Macbeth *seem* horrified at Duncan's murder.

WHAT TO DO

There are many examples of this kind in the play. Can you continue the list in the same way?

Here are some hints to help you find the examples: In your list, mark which is which with an A or a B.

   a dagger   a wood   false promises

   a ghost   two guilty grooms   a wicked prince

   a 'foul and fair' day

A. Sometimes we, the audience, know that the appearance is different from the reality before some of the characters.

B. Sometimes we are in the dark just like them, and discover later what the truth is.

DARKNESS . . .

The work on these two pages is to help you look more closely at the way Shakespeare's language affects an audience as much as the events in the play.

1. *Macbeth* was first performed indoors, in front of a small audience.
2. In Shakespeare's time there was, of course, no electric light; the play-room would have been lit by candles. If you've ever been in a place lit only by candles, you'll know that they give bright spots of light, and deep shadows that move as people move past the candles. (Candle light also affects the way faces appear - half in light, half in shadow.)
3. You remember that some of the most important events in *Macbeth* take place in darkness: the murder of Duncan, the murder of Banquo, Macbeth's visit to the witches, and Lady Macbeth's sleep-walking. Shakespeare chose to do this deliberately - it's not hard to think why.
4. Many of the characters mention darkness as the play goes on. The repetition of word-images of dark and night feeds our imaginations, so that we never forget for long, even while reading the play in broad daylight, that darkness hangs over the play. Here are some examples:

(Macbeth thinking about killing Duncan - Act 1, Scene 5, line 50 -)
> Come, thick night,
> And pall thee in the dimmest smoke of hell,
> That my keen knife see not the wound it makes,
> Nor heaven peep through the blanket of the dark,
> To cry "Hold, hold!"

(Banquo, just before the murder - Act 2, Scene 1, line 5)
> There's husbandry in heaven.
> Their candles are all out."

5. Shakespeare also gives us word-pictures of darkness *struggling* with light, and darkness winning. When this is repeated, it creates a feeling, or *atmosphere* in the play which we can remember even when we have forgotten the words themselves:

(Macbeth thinking about killing Duncan - Act 1, Scene 4, line 50)
> Stars, hide your fires.
> Let not light see my black and deep desires.

WHAT TO DO

Talk about these images together. Do you understand what they mean? For example, what does "dark night strangles the travelling lamp" mean? What do the words "Light thickens" mean to you?
When you have discussed them, copy out each quotation and write notes on the meanings you arrive at in your discussion.

Notes on Darkness in MACBETH

Indoors - small audience

Candle light - deep shadows
     spooky!

Important scenes in MACBETH
in the dark : Murder of Dunc.
          Murder of Banquo
     MACB's visit to witches

Shakes. deliberate - it's a
               dark play!

Darkness mentioned a lot.

repeated word-images of
dark and night - feeds the
                    imagination.

Lady Macb - 1.5.50
     "Come, thick night..."

Darkness struggles with light,
Light wins.
Atmosphere - because always
               repeated.

"Stars hide your fires." 1.4.50

"Dark night strangles the
   travellers lamp" 3.4.46
          |
          Sun??

"nights black agents" - good
     quote. Could say Macb.
     & Lady Macb. are ----

AND DISEASE

There is another chain of images in the play which deal this time with disease. They create an atmosphere in which Scotland is like a healthy body which contains a deadly disease - Macbeth - waiting to break out. These are the references for the images:

1,3,23 — Who is causing this sickness?
2,2,45 — Why does Lady Macbeth tell Macbeth his brain is sick?
3,4,87 — Why does Macbeth lie like this?
4,3,214 — How is Macduff's revenge like a medicine?
5,1,62 — Why is this disease beyond the Doctor to cure?
5,2,26 — How will Scotland be cured?

WHAT TO DO

A. Look up each reference. Copy out the line/s which contain the image of disease.
B. Make sure you understand what each one means, by talking about them. Again write notes on your discussion.
C. You can use your notes as the basis of an essay on imagery in *Macbeth*.

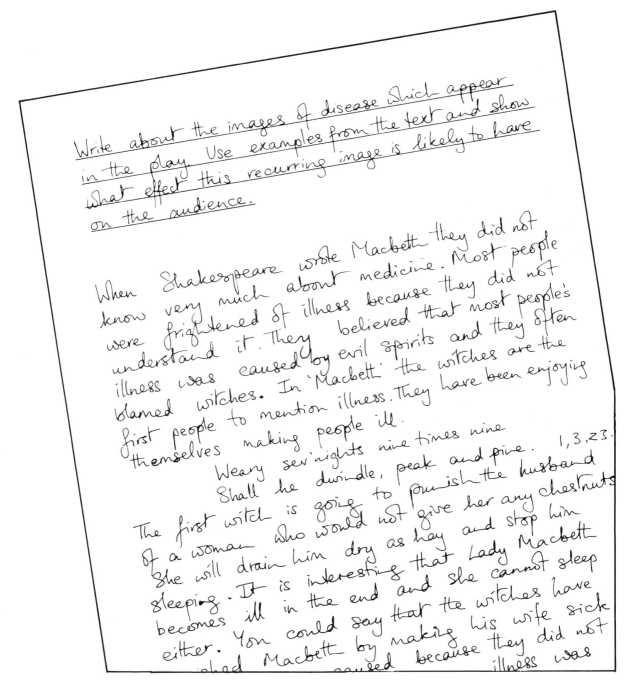

Write about the images of disease which appear in the play. Use examples from the text and show what effect this recurring image is likely to have on the audience.

When Shakespeare wrote Macbeth they did not know very much about medicine. Most people were frightened of illness because they did not understand it. They believed that most people's illness was caused by evil spirits and they often blamed witches. In 'Macbeth' the witches are the first people to mention illness. They have been enjoying themselves making people ill.

Weary sev'nights nine times nine
Shall he dwindle, peak and pine.   1,3,23.

The first witch is going to punish the husband of a woman who would not give her any chestnuts. She will drain him dry as hay and stop him sleeping. It is interesting that Lady Macbeth becomes ill in the end and she cannot sleep either. You could say that the witches have ... ed Macbeth by making his wife sick ... ... ed because they did not illness was

45

LOOKING CLOSELY AT ONE SCENE

METHOUGHT I HEARD A VOICE CRY, 'SLEEP NO MORE!'

In the course of the play, although Macbeth manages to sleep, we learn that he is afflicted by 'terrible dreams' after he has murdered Duncan. And he is not the only one. Lady Macbeth suffers too; we see her walking in her sleep and going over in her mind what she has done. Even in her sleep, her deeds are not forgotten.

Lady Macbeth's sleep-walking statements are very confusing to the Doctor and Waiting Woman, but we know they refer to various things that have happened in the play, though not in the right order. Lady Macbeth is speaking a nightmare out loud, and these are some of the things she says:

a) One; two; why, then tis time to do't.

b) Fie, my lord, fie! A soldier, and afeard?

c) Who would have thought the old man to have had so much blood in him?

d) The Thane of Fife had a wife. Where is she now?

e) No more o' that, my lord, no more o' that! You mar all this with starting.

f) I tell you yet again, Banquo's buried. He cannot come out on's grave.

g) To bed, to bed! There's knocking at the gate.

h) What's done cannot be undone. To bed, to bed, to bed.

WHAT TO DO

1. Can you remember what earlier incidents each of these statements refer to?
   For example: a) - This refers to the ringing of the bell which was the sign for Macbeth to murder Duncan.

2. Now see if you can find the exact references in the play. Most of the incidents she refers to are in Act 1 Scene 7 and Act 2 Scene 2, but there are some references to other places.
   For example: a) - This refers to the lines: 2,31,32.:
   Go bid thy mistress, when my drink is ready,
   She strike upon the bell.

3. Why does Shakespeare select these particular fragme to repeat in this scene?
   Why do you think Shakespeare has the Doctor and Waiting Woman in this scene at all?

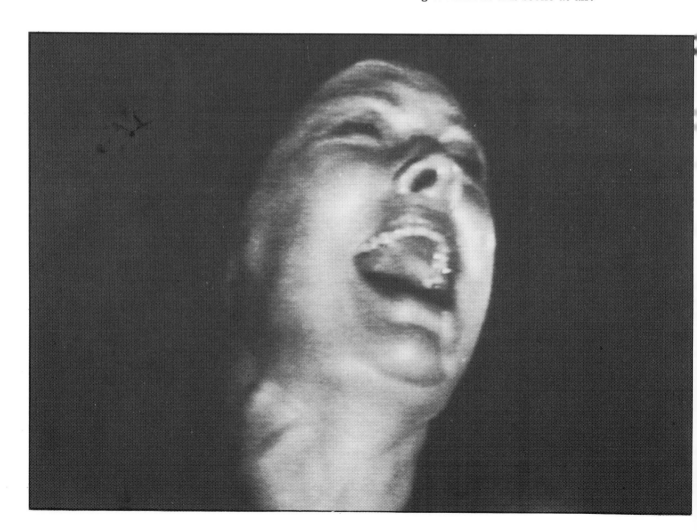

QUIZ

TRY THIS QUIZ WITH SOMEONE ELSE.
THE ANSWERS ARE ON PAGE 48.

EASY

1. What has Macbeth done to please King Duncan?

2. How many of the witches' first three predictions come true?

3. Why is the porter so slow in answering the door?

4. Why does Macbeth behave so strangely at the banquet?

5. Why does Birnam Wood appear to move?

MEDIUM

6. What are Macbeth's first words in the play?

7. What three names do the witches call Macbeth by?

8. How does Lady Macbeth put the guilt for Duncan's murder onto his servants?

9. Why do Malcolm and Donalbain hurry away from Scotland?

0. What argument does Macbeth use to convince the murderers that they should kill Banquo?

1. Why is Macbeth furious that Fleance escaped?

2. Can you name any four things the witches put in their cauldron?

3. Which two people see Lady Macbeth walking in her sleep?

4. Who becomes King at the end of the play?

HARD

5. What makes Duncan believe Macbeth's castle is a pleasant place?

6. Why does Lady Macbeth say she could not kill Duncan herself?

7. Why is one of the witches angry with a sailor's wife?

8. How many kings appear to Macbeth when he asks the witches whether Banquo's sons will rule Scotland?

9. Who tells Lady Macduff she should try to escape?

0. Whom do we see Macbeth kill in the final battle?

WHO SAID — TO WHOM — WHEN?

1.   Doubtful it stood,
   As two spent swimmers that do cling together
   And choke their art. *(1,2)*

2. So well thy words become thee as thy wounds:
   They smack of honour both *(1,2)*

3. Here I have a pilot's thumb,
   Wracked as homeward he did come. *(1,3)*

4. What, can the devil speak true? *(1,3)*

5.   Come what may,
   Time and the hour runs through the roughest day *(1,3)*

6. Your face, my Thane, is as a book where men
   May read strange matters *(1,5)*

You might like to choose another Act in the play and make a similar quiz for other people in your group
to answer.

QUIZ ANSWERS

EASY

1. He has killed the rebel, Macdonald.
2. All three.
3. Because he is drunk.
4. Because he can see the ghost of Banquo. No-one else can see it.
5. Because each soldier is carrying the branch of a tree to disguise how many of them there are.

MEDIUM

6. "So foul and fair a day I have not seen."
7. Thane of Glamis, Thane of Cawdor, King.
8. By smearing the blood from the daggers onto the servants as they sleep.
9. Because they feel that whoever murdered Duncan may turn on them next.
10. Macbeth tells the murderers that Banquo is responsible for making them and their families poor.
11. Because Fleance is Banquo's son, and the witches said that Banquo's sons would be kings.
12. See the speeches in Act 4, Scene 1, lines 5-38.
13. A Doctor and a waiting-woman (one of Lady Macbeth's personal servants).
14. Malcolm.

HARD

15. The castle has a pleasant setting, and the fact that swifts build their nests in the castle is a sign that the climate is healthy.
16. Because he looked like her father.
17. Because the sailor's wife would not give her some of the chestnuts she was eating.
18. Eight (see Act 4, Scene 1, lines 110-125).
19. The nobleman, Ross, and a messenger who is not named.
20. Young Siward, Malcolm's cousin.

WHO SAID — TO WHOM — WHEN

1. The Captain telling Duncan and his court about the battle against the rebels at the beginning of the play.
2. Duncan thanking the Captain for his news.
3. First witch to the other witches while they wait for Macbeth.
4. Banquo to Ross, Angus and Macbeth on hearing that Macbeth has been made Thane of Cawdor as the witches predicted.
5. Macbeth to himself about the idea that he might become King. Said while Banquo waits.
6. Lady Macbeth to Macbeth after she has suggested that they murder Duncan.